CONVERGE
Bible Studies

OUR COMMON SINS

Bible Studies

OUR COMMON SINS

DOTTIE ESCOBEDO-FRANK

Abingdon Press

Nashville

OUR COMMON SINS
CONVERGE BIBLE STUDIES

By Dottie Escobedo-Frank

Library of Congress Cataloging-in-Publication Data has been requested.

ISBN: 978-1-4267-6898-9

Series Editor: Shane Raynor

13 14 15 16 17 18 19 20 21 22—10 9 8 7 6 5 4 3 2 1

Manufactured in the United States of America

CONTENTS

ABOUT THE SERIES

Converge is a new series of topical Bible studies based on the Common English Bible translation. Each title in the *Converge* series consists of four studies based around a common topic or theme. *Converge* brings together a unique group of writers from different backgrounds, traditions, and age groups.

HOW TO USE THESE STUDIES

Converge Bible studies can be used by small groups, classes, or individuals. Each study uses a simple format. For the convenience of the reader, the primary Scripture passages are included. In Insight and Ideas, the author of the study guide explores each Scripture passage, going deeper into the text and helping readers understand how the Scripture connects with the theme of the study. Questions are designed to encourage both personal reflection and group conversation. Some questions may not have simple answers. That's part of what makes studying the Bible so exciting.

Although Bible passages are included with each session, study participants may find it useful to have personal Bibles on hand for referencing other Scriptures. *Converge* studies are designed for use with the Common English Bible; but they work well with any modern, reliable translation.

ONLINE EXTRAS

Converge studies are available in both print and digital formats. Each title in the series has additional components that are available online, including companion articles, blog posts, extra questions, sermon ideas, and podcasts.

To access the companion materials, visit

http://www.MinistryMatters.com/Converge

Thanks for using *Converge*!

INTRODUCTION

They loved him. Jesus had become more than their guide; he was now their friend. He had changed from an associate to the one they would give their life for. Jesus had wormed his way into their hearts so much that their lives were no longer the same. And he loved them. He loved them when they didn't understand who he was. He loved them when they denied him, when they slept through crucial times, when they lied, and when they betrayed him.

Nothing, *no*-thing, stopped Jesus from loving them; and so they came to love him in return.

These original disciples were fairly ordinary folk. They had regular families, they made their livelihoods in regular ways, and they had typical and varied political leanings. But they met Jesus and started to live extraordinary lives. The disciples watched the sick healed and the demon-possessed set free. They saw a few fish and loaves of bread feed thousands of people. They watched the storm be calmed. They saw love transferred to the women, the children, and the otherwise "outcasts" of their day. These things made them ordinary people living an extraordinary life experience.

But because of their closeness to Jesus, we tend to think that they lived lives with less . . . um . . . well, with less "sin" than we live with. We imagine Jesus' perfect love rubbed off on them perfectly so that they were also extraordinary humans. But the Gospels show us different. They show us that Jesus' close companions were as human as you and I. And it startles us when we see ourselves reflected in the disciples of the Gospel story. The Gospel of Mark tells the story with power, bluntness, and a sense of urgency.

You see, the Gospel of Mark was the first. It was the first written narrative of Jesus' life in the newly formed faith community of Christians. This Gospel was used as a source for two other Gospels: Matthew and Luke. And we think that it's possible, even probable, that this Gospel was written during the persecution of Christians by Nero (A.D. 64), which would include the Jewish uprising against Rome. Perhaps that is why Mark's Gospel focuses on the difficulties Jesus and his followers faced in their daily lives.

Mark has two endings. The first ending is the one found in the oldest texts, and the second ending was perhaps added later. Although we tend to like the second ending better, the first ending is important: Jesus' followers have lost their nerve and are running away from the empty tomb, both terrified and silenced. While they're told to "Go, tell his disciples . . . " (Mark 16:7a), they instead say nothing to anyone, because they're afraid. The first ending is remarkably candid. Death and unexpected empty tombs scare the bejeebers out of us. The first ending shadows much of our reactions to surprise—even to good news. Because good news doesn't always come in pretty and predictable packages, and because good news often has a sprinkle of bad news in it, "Jesus has risen!" comes with the soul-rattling "Jesus died." We often don't know what to make of the things that challenge our ordinary living and thinking.

The disciples had to learn this over and over. They failed often, even when their teacher was standing right there with them to guide them. They made their mistakes in front of the Master, the one they loved dearly. Most of us want to impress our teachers, so we quickly learn to keep our mouths shut rather than say something stupid in class that will be corrected in front of all of our friends. Most students become experts at not failing, which means we become novices at risk-taking boldness. But these disciples failed over and over in front of Jesus, in front of one another, and in front of the whole world—even spanning thousands of years as we're still reading about their mistakes. The thing is, not many in the world are making fun of them. Their mistakes and failings make us uncomfortable and cause us to squirm in our seats, because, well . . . because they hit so close to home. We can't laugh at someone else if we would've done the exact same thing or worse.

What if, for example, you were there when Jesus said, "Here, hand out this bread and fish to the crowds. You feed them." Would you have laughed at Jesus? Would you have scoffed, mocked, and walked away in disgust at Jesus' request? Maybe. Or maybe you would've thought that Jesus was losing it—too much preaching in the sun without water. What thoughts, words, and actions would we have to repent of had we been the ones handing out the fish and loaves?

It is because we recognize the sins of the disciples as our own that we can relate to them so closely. They are our common sins. We hope that we can learn from what they experienced. We, too, deny Christ when our coworker sneers, "So are you one of those 'born-again' fools?" We, too, sleep through really important world events when we should be on our knees in deep, agonizing prayer. We, too, lie, bring false testimony about Jesus when we proclaim him while living a life that's not like his. We, too, betray him to his very own death while we attempt to prove that we're godlike. The disciples are us; we are them.

We have so much to learn, and this journey is not for the timid. It will call on all of the courage you can muster in your soul. I am hoping that you are ready to dig deep, to find the ways we sin along with the disciples; and then I'm hoping that you'll be willing to be set free from everything that binds you. For it is only when we are unloosed that we begin to live extraordinarily.

1

DENIAL
LIVING UNFAITHFULLY

SCRIPTURE
MARK 14:27-31, 66-72

[27]Jesus said to them, "You will all falter in your faithfulness to me. It is written, *I will hit the shepherd, and the sheep will go off in all directions.* [28]But after I'm raised up, I will go before you to Galilee."

[29]Peter said to him, "Even if everyone else stumbles, I won't."

[30]But Jesus said to him, "I assure you that on this very night, before the rooster crows twice, you will deny me three times."

[31]But Peter insisted, "If I must die alongside you, I won't deny you." And they all said the same thing.

***

[66]Meanwhile, Peter was below in the courtyard. A woman, one of the high priest's servants, approached [67]and saw Peter warming

himself by the fire. She stared at him and said, "You were also with the Nazarene, Jesus."

68But he denied it, saying, "I don't know what you're talking about. I don't understand what you're saying." And he went outside into the outer courtyard. A rooster crowed.

69The female servant saw him and began a second time to say to those standing around, "This man is one of them." 70But he denied it again.

A short time later, those standing around again said to Peter, "You must be one of them, because you are also a Galilean."

71But he cursed and swore, "I don't know this man you're talking about." 72At that very moment, a rooster crowed a second time. Peter remembered what Jesus told him, "Before a rooster crows twice, you will deny me three times." And he broke down, sobbing.

INSIGHT AND IDEAS

Of course, we think, *we* wouldn't have done that. In Jesus' lowest hours, we would have remained faithful. I'll never forget when a non-follower friend of mine read this story about Peter. She said, "Man, Peter's on my _____ list! He just ignored his homey in trouble." (Later, when she read more of Peter's life story after the Resurrection, she said that she was forgiving him. Peter was redeeming himself.) While I laughed at her honest reaction to hearing a story for the first time (something that I wish we all could do now and then), she nailed our feelings about Peter's denial.

We, of course, would *never* treat a friend and or family member in such a way—especially if he had just been arrested and was facing death. *We* would never wonder whether he actually caused this to happen to himself. *We* would never blame the victim when he was down. *We* would never *not* claim a close personal relationship with a convict. Do you sense my tongue-in-cheek questioning? The truth is, we sure would like to think that we would be better than Peter in this situation; but the reason we connect with him so much is that we know that we're really so much like him. And that realization hurts.

Simon had gone through a life transformation, and part of it was a name change. His Lord called him "Peter" (*Petros*, meaning *rock*). Jesus was saying that Simon would now be Peter, faithful, "solid-as-a-rock." I wonder whether Simon laughed inwardly when Jesus renamed him. He knew himself to be a volatile, emotional, speak-before-you-think person. He must have been surprised by Jesus' call-out to faithfulness and by the new person he was becoming.

And that's why this denial hurt so much. He failed in faithfulness. He failed to be strong as a rock when his world was crumbling. He failed to stand up for his beloved friend and teacher.

On occasion, I've heard people talk negatively about professors or preachers I know and love. These detractors are unaware that I look to the ones they're criticizing as mentors. When the bashing begins, something inside me wilts because I can't believe that not everyone sees my mentors as I do. Our faith is tested at these wilting places. It is here that we have a choice—to speak out and stand in our connection; remain silent by changing the conversation; or worse, agree through our snickers and laughter. When we arrive at this decision place, we find out that we aren't always different from Peter.

We must acknowledge, of course, the difficult place Peter was in. Because of association, he too could have been arrested. He knew that they were out to kill Jesus, and Peter was trying to save his own skin. We understand the difficulty of that choice. But from the passage, it seems that Peter didn't even think about his answer; he just quickly and succinctly denied that he knew Jesus. He had a knee-jerk reaction of denial.

Faithful. Jesus had called him a rock. But in this moment, Peter was more like quicksand. He was sinking fast.

First, a woman who worked for the high priest (the leader of the group who wanted to kill Jesus) noticed Peter as he was getting warm by the fire. She eagle-stared him and said, "You were also with the Nazarene, Jesus."

Peter just denied it fervently, "I don't know what you're talking about. I don't understand what you're saying." Then he took off into the outside courtyard while a rooster crowed in the background.

The second time, the same woman saw him again, this time proclaiming to the crowd, "This man is one of them."

Peter must've been thinking, *Who is this woman and why won't she leave me alone?* Then he said again out loud that he didn't know what she was talking about.

The third time, people were standing around; and someone said directly to Peter, "You must be one of them, because you are also a Galilean."

This time, Peter showed his best colors by swearing and cursing. And he stated vehemently, "I don't know this man you're talking about."

Peter's temper flared to full height and full-on rage. And right when he was about to explode in anger. . . .

The rooster crowed again.

It crowed so that Peter could remember Jesus' words: "I assure you that on this very night, before the rooster crows twice, you will deny me three times."

It crowed so that Peter could recall his quick response, "If I must die alongside you, I won't deny you."

And it crowed twice so that Peter could feel the full weight of his denial.

And Peter broke down and bucket-sobbed. The rock crumbled into a sorrowing pit. He cried bucket-tears of remorse for letting himself down. Bucket-tears of love for a friend who had never deserted him. Bucket-tears of a broken-hearted man.

Peter cried out for repentance and help and transformation. He cried to regain his status as the faithful rock. He cried for a restored relationship with Jesus.

Have you ever been unfaithful to your Savior? Have you ever denied Christ Jesus, your Lord?

I know that I have. It is my greatest sin. As a young woman, I became the mother of a baby girl who died at four days of age. I prepared for her death; but when it came, I was stunned nonetheless. I couldn't believe that I would have to lose my child. And in my stunned and listless state, I gave up on God. As I watched my infant daughter's casket being lowered into the ground, I buried God there too. I quit believing. I quit hoping. I quit caring. I existed in a state of unbelief. I found out how lonely it is to be without God.

During this time, I went to church because my husband pestered me to go. I went through my daily routine, alive on the outside but dead on the inside. I finished classes, worked, and ate. But there was little life left in me.

Then one day, a miracle came into our lives in the form of another child. And when Sara was laid in my hands, I experienced God's great love. I suddenly knew that God had never left me. I knew that God had never believed in my unbelief. I knew that God had saved me from myself.

It took me years to forgive myself for my unfaithfulness to God. And while today, many years later, I can understand how grief and pain does this to a person, I am still working to be faithful, strong, and a source of hope to others. I understand Peter's tears, because they are mine too.

You may not have had such a dramatic experience of denial. Maybe yours is more about the silence in the face of a crowd that jeers at Jesus. Maybe yours is the experience of pretending you don't go to church, or denying that faith can change things in your life. Maybe your experience is the subtle, constant neglect of the love that was once your lifeline.

I think that Peter's tears gave him his life back. Tears are healing and faithful. They are the mechanism God uses to allow us to enter into the flow of God. In Bible days, and later, in Victorian times, tears were seen as so precious that they were collected in bottles. Psalm 56:8 says,

> You yourself have kept track of my misery.
>   Put my tears into your bottle—
>   aren't they on your scroll already?

This Scripture points out that our tears so precious that they are God's collectible items. This tradition carried on into the Victorian times, when a stopper was added to the bottle. Tears of grief were collected and added to as an outward sign of an inward pain. Since pain often comes from the loss of a love, tears are actually an outward sign of an inward love. Paying attention to our tears brings healing, cleanses us of our sins, and reconnects us to the One we love. And Peter was healed of his faithlessness and his denial.

We know that Peter was healed because of his life. He went on to establish churches in Antioch and preached all over the known world. He wrote letters to faith communities. He spread the gospel. People were healed when Peter prayed. Even his shadow brought healing.

We believe that Peter died at the hands of Nero, and tradition has it that he was crucified upside down because he said that he didn't deserve to die the same way his Lord had died. In the end, Peter proclaimed Jesus with his life and in his death. He was the Rock, the faithful one, once again.

And so, from a distance, we see the whole picture. There may be times in our lives when we deny that we know, or that we love, Jesus Christ our Lord. Those times will bring us great pain and sorrow and will cause us to make a choice. The choice is this: Will we continue to live unfaithfully, or will we learn from our common sins and make something beautiful of our mistakes? This choice comes daily. It comes in our decisions about whom to love, where to connect to a church community, how we work, what we say, and when we're silent. The choice, daily made, is still ours.

I have a friend whom I call the Encourager. When I am struggling with something in the church, I call him and explain what's going on; and he listens and gives a little feedback. But mostly, he ends every conversation with "Be encouraged." It's his way of reminding me that

God is faithful and that we can be faithful too. This encouragement is really what we need now.

We will cry, but I'm thinking that we can make beauty out of tears. We can turn our common sins into deep understanding of God's grace because Jesus died and rose so that we could know the depth of God's love. This means that you are *beloved* in God's sight. This means that you are *beautiful* to the Maker. This means that your *truthfulness* shines like a light in the darkest room.

I'm thinking that we can take our common sin of *denial* and turn it into *faithful* to the end.

QUESTIONS

1. Why does Jesus tell the disciples that they will leave him? Is he locking them into a course of failure when he gives them this information?

2. How would you respond if you were one of the disciples and Jesus had said this to you?

3. The Greek word translated *falter* in verse 27 is *skandalizo,* which is related to the English word *scandalize*. How are the actions of Jesus' disciples in Mark 14 scandalous?

4. Galilee is mentioned twice, once by Jesus (verse 28) and once by one of the crowd in the outer courtyard (verse 70). What is the significance of Galilee? Is there a connection between the two references?

5. Why, do you think, is Peter so confident that he won't abandon Jesus?

6. What might be going through Peter's mind when he hears the first rooster crow in verse 68? Why doesn't Peter remember what Jesus said before hearing the second rooster crow?

7. Why does Peter decide to save himself? What does this say about *our* desire to save ourselves?

8. Why is it so easy for twenty-first century readers to judge Peter for denying Jesus?

9. In what ways do we deny Christ today? In what ways do we deny our fellow Christians?

10. How should we handle the grief that we often experience after we're unfaithful to God?

2

SLEEPING THROUGH IMPORTANCE
FAILING TO BE THERE

SCRIPTURE
MARK 14:32-42

[32]Jesus and his disciples came to a place called Gethsemane. Jesus said to them, "Sit here while I pray." [33]He took Peter, James, and John along with him. He began to feel despair and was anxious. [34]He said to them, "I'm very sad. It's as if I'm dying. Stay here and keep alert." [35]Then he went a short distance farther and fell to the ground. He prayed that, if possible, he might be spared the time of suffering. [36]He said, "Abba, Father, for you all things are possible. Take this cup of suffering away from me. However—not what I want but what you want."

[37]He came and found them sleeping. He said to Peter, "Simon, are you asleep? Couldn't you stay alert for one hour? [38]Stay alert and pray so that you won't give in to temptation. The spirit is eager, but the flesh is weak."

[39]Again, he left them and prayed, repeating the same words. [40]And, again, when he came back, he found them sleeping, for they couldn't keep their eyes open, and they didn't know how to respond to him. [41]He came a third time and said to them, "Will you sleep and rest all night? That's enough! The time has come for the Human One to be betrayed into the hands of sinners. [42]Get up! Let's go! Look, here comes my betrayer."

INSIGHT AND IDEAS

It's really embarrassing when we sleep through important, life-changing, even agonizing moments. It's even embarrassing when we sleep through not-so-important things. It tells our companions that they aren't important, and it takes a while to get over the loud and clear nonverbal message that was given.

Once I slept through a date. My high school sweetheart had taken me to a movie. This was when movies were shown in outdoor theaters, and the car had a speaker attached to the window. It was really a time for the town teenagers to get together, eat hot dogs and popcorn, and party. But inside the car, during a movie whose title I can still remember, I fell sound asleep. At the end of the movie, my date woke me up and pouted all the way home while I apologized. It took about a week of apologies before he forgave me. He was glad to be with me; I was obviously not in the same frame of mind.

I recall one other event when I watched someone sleep through an important conversation. I was a social work student intern and was accompanying a physician intern to give the bad news to a mother that her little child had been abused by someone in the home. Really, really tough news to hear. The physician intern had been up for thirty-something hours and let me know that he was very tired.

We went into the room together to talk with the mother. We were sitting close together in a small room with three small desks crammed in the space. The physician intern began to explain the injuries and went on to tell the frightened mother that these could occur only through abuse . . . that her child was being abused by someone. I was watching mom's face, and I saw the devastation cross her eyes as she took it all in.

And then there was silence.

I was still looking at her face, but the silence went on too long; and then mom's expression changed. I looked over at the physician intern. He had his face propped up on his hand and was sound asleep. Right after delivering the bad news, he fell asleep in our presence.

The mom was so shaken up by his words and then by his inattentiveness to her problem, that she began to cry. I shook his arm until he woke up, and he apologized profusely. But the damage was done. He slept through something really important. It made a painful moment even worse.

Jesus needed to get before God and pray; and he chose his closest friends, Peter, James, and John, to go with him. He explained to them that he was in deep sorrow and even felt his body close to death for the weight of his experience. He needed them to stay close by, awake, and alert; and he needed them to take care of him as he faced his hour of pain.

He was so upset that he threw himself on the floor. Have you ever been so distraught that you lay on the bathroom floor, away from everyone else, and just cried out to God? Or have you been alone in the house, face on the ground, groaning out your pain? That's where Jesus was, except the weight of his pain was the knowledge that his death was near. He could even feel it in his body. He cried out to God to save him from this pain if it were possible, at the same time telling his Father that he would still go through this trial if it was God's will. Jesus' spirit went through an agonizing fight against the moment and simple surrender, all at the same time.

He went to call on his friends for help, but they were sound asleep. He said to Peter, "Simon, are you asleep? Couldn't you stay alert for one hour? Stay alert and pray so that you won't give in to temptation. The spirit is eager, but the flesh is weak."

He was saying to Peter to at least pray for himself if he couldn't pray for Jesus. He scolded his inattentive, sleepy friend because he was not present in Jesus' time of need.

Jesus went away to pray again, repeating his prayer from before. As we often do, Jesus said the same thing over and over. (Sometimes it's really all we have to say, and we want to make sure we're heard.) When he was done, he reached out again for the support of his friends and found them sleeping. They didn't know what to say to Jesus. They could see agony on his face and lack of peace in his body, but their love wasn't strong enough to stay awake. They were silenced by their own lack of caring.

The ministry of presence is often all we have to give during times of deep grief and sorrow. Anyone who has lost a loved one knows that there are no words that can bring comfort or lighten the sorrow. Words are inadequate, trite, and often unintentionally hurtful. But what is remembered is presence—that someone you loved showed up at the awful moments of life. That speaks volumes.

The midnight visitor who hops on a plane to spend three hours with a mama and papa whose child is dying, and then returns home on the 4:00 A.M. flight, speaks volumes. The friend who shows up to say a few words at a funeral service speaks volumes. The woman who brings over tea and a gift then sits silently, just holding your hand and listening—that speaks volumes. The presence of a friend during difficulty cements that friendship.

Jesus was asking for the ministry of presence to be directed his way, but it didn't happen. And so he did the very next best thing: He demanded the presence of his friends in the upcoming moment of pain. For he knew that as they experienced his beloved betrayer turning on him, they too would know the importance of the moment. They would learn about the ministry of presence whether they wanted to or not.

Jesus went away and prayed for the third time and then came back to them, this time saying, "Will you sleep and rest all night? That's enough! The time has come for the Human One to be betrayed into the hands of sinners. Get up! Let's go! Look, here comes my betrayer."

You can see that after three times of being deserted by his friends in his time of need (and after all of the times Jesus had been there for them when they needed him), Jesus has a change of tone. He becomes directive and tells them that they are done with sleeping. Even if they don't get it, he warns them that—right now—Jesus' betrayer is on his way. And Jesus is determined for them to be wide awake during this encounter. How else will they understand what's coming if they don't experience it for themselves? How will they know the significance of his betrayal if they sleep through this important moment? How else will they feel his agony unless they're present and awake?

Sometimes we need to be awakened to the reality of life. We're not called to sleep through moments of importance; we're called to be fully alive to the good and the not-so-good that is our experience. The disciples learned that day that wakefulness to life (and death) was required to follow Jesus.

So, what important things have you been sleeping through? Are you ignoring the deep end while remaining in the shallow waters of the pool of life? Are you sleeping through importance?

The average person, who lives to the age of 75 and sleeps eight hours a night, sleeps 219,000 hours in a lifetime. That means that 438,000 hours in a lifetime are spent awake. But to be awake two-thirds of one's lifetime means that we're fully engaged in the living. Are we fully engaged when we're zoned out on TV or videogames? Are we fully engaged when our only friends are in the cyber world of social media? Are we fully engaged when we spend our evenings connected to computers but ignoring the fully human person in the same room with us?

Sometimes we zone out of living because we're afraid of what we might encounter in life. Sometimes we zone out because we're truly weary of life's lessons. Sometimes we zone out because we've never been given the tools to deal with the realities of living. It's easier to ignore, pretend, and stay in the shallow waters of a relationship. It's easier to pretend we don't know that there are hunger, abuse, and loneliness in the world. It's easier to pretend that the homeless don't live in our neighborhoods—or worse, to say that they all "deserve" the life they're living.

It's harder to fully encounter another person. In some ways it is easier to encounter the stranger, because there's no requirement of commitment. But when we love someone, even when we love someone who's so different from us, then it's hard to stay engaged. The most difficult person to love is the one you love so much. Now that's the hard stuff!

But the most hopeful words come from 1 Corinthians 13:12, which describes the perfection of heaven and the perfect relationship:

> Now we see a reflection in a mirror; then we will see face-to-face. Now I know partially, but then I will know completely in the same way that I have been completely known.

Heaven on earth's possibilities lie in our ability to fully encounter life and death with one another. They lie in our ability to remain present. They lie in our staying awake through one another's trials and temptations.

We just have to remember the tenderness that comes when we force ourselves to stay awake in those middle-of-the-night experiences. As a mom or dad, perhaps you've responded to your baby's 2:00 A.M. cries of hunger. Although you're tired, you force yourself awake and pick up your beautiful, crying child. You heat up the bottle and pat her back while counting the seconds until the milk is warmed. Then you go to your favorite rocking chair, and your baby sucks hungrily, making little sounds of joy. She is wide awake; looks up at you with unveiled eyes of love; and says, "I love you!" with her twinkling eyes. And then your little midnight crier reaches up her little hands and touches your face with her soft fingers. Then you realize that the midnight encounters are the ones you'll remember forever.

And for this, we must stay awake.

QUESTIONS

1. Why does Jesus take only three of the disciples with him to pray (verse 33)? Why does he choose Peter, James, and John?

Closest friends

2. Verse 33 says that Jesus begins to feel deep despair and anxiety. How can we find reassurance in this information?

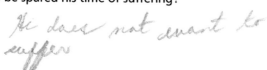

Humaness

3. Why does Jesus fall to the ground in verse 35? Why does he pray to be spared his time of suffering?

He does not want to suffer

4. Jesus states in verse 36 that all things are possible with the Father, then he asks that the cup of suffering be taken from him. What crucial part of God's plan does Christ's suffering fulfill?

For our sins

5. In verse 36, Jesus prays to the Father, "Not what I want but what you want." What conclusions, if any, can we draw about the will of the Son and its connection to the will of the Father?

The will of the father is to be met

6. What is the temptation that Jesus refers to in verse 38?

Sleep

7. What does Jesus mean when he says, "The spirit is eager but the flesh is weak" in verse 38?

he wish to do our best

8. Verse 39 tells us that Jesus prays again, repeating the same words as before. What can we learn about prayer from this detail?

asking the same things over and over

9. Is Jesus scolding the disciples in this passage? What clues do we have about the emotions Jesus might be experiencing when he confronts the sleeping disciples? Why does he single out Peter in verse 37 when the others are asleep too?

He is supposed to be the best friend & rock.

10. Verse 40 says that the disciples didn't know how to respond to Jesus. How would you have responded to him in their situation?

Probably the same.

11. Sometimes the ministry of presence is all we have to offer someone else when he or she is going through a difficult time. Why is this ministry so important?

Not to be suffering alone.

12. What steps can we take to make sure that we're able to be there for others when they need us most?

Being faithful & compassionate friends.

3

TELLING LIES
AVOIDING THE TRUTH

SCRIPTURE
MARK 14:53-65

[53]They led Jesus away to the high priest, and all the chief priests, elders, and legal experts gathered. [54]Peter followed him from a distance, right into the high priest's courtyard. He was sitting with the guards, warming himself by the fire. [55]The chief priests and the whole Sanhedrin were looking for testimony against Jesus in order to put him to death, but they couldn't find any. [56]Many brought false testimony against him, but they contradicted each other. [57]Some stood to offer false witness against him, saying, [58]"We heard him saying, 'I will destroy this temple, constructed by humans, and within three days I will build another, one not made by humans.'" [59]But their testimonies didn't agree even on this point.

[60]Then the high priest stood up in the middle of the gathering and examined Jesus. "Aren't you going to respond to the testimony

these people have brought against you?" [61]But Jesus was silent and didn't answer. Again, the high priest asked, "Are you the Christ, the Son of the blessed one?"

[62]Jesus said, "I am. And you will see the Human One sitting on the right side of the Almighty and coming on the heavenly clouds."

[63]Then the high priest tore his clothes and said, "Why do we need any more witnesses? [64]You've heard his insult against God. What do you think?"

They all condemned him. "He deserves to die!"

[65]Some began to spit on him. Some covered his face and hit him, saying, "Prophesy!" Then the guards took him and beat him.

INSIGHT AND IDEAS

I was very surprised when I went through an experience of people lying about me. Of course, like most people, there had been little lies and rumors that were part of the growing-up experience: Someone takes what you said and passes it on out of context, a person makes up a lie about you out of anger, or someone's exaggeration gets blown out of proportion. And I, too, had played the game of "telephone" or "gossip" as a child; so I knew that lying, even unintentionally, is very easy to do. Our ears are selective; and sometimes they're tuned in to the juicy, wild stories more than to common sense. All that was normal, and I understood it.

But this was different. These were downright lies, made-up facts to fit a need, taking a little kernel of truth and twisting it to give a message. We had begun to feed the homeless on our church property; and after some time, a small group of neighbors got upset that the homeless were on our land, which was close to their homes. So they protested to the city. The city gave us a cease and desist order; thus we began a long, drawn-out battle, including public hearings.

We made an attempt to talk with our neighbors. The problem, however, wasn't our neighbors in general, but a select group of neighbors who took many of their daytime and some nighttime hours to spread lies. They wrote letters about how terrible I, the pastor, was in leading the church down the wrong path and posted the letters on car windshields during Sunday worship. They caused a verbal fight in the parking lot on the same Sunday, and the police showed up to settle things down.

E-mail blasts were sent out to the neighborhood association, accusing me of telling lies; and stories were told that were simply untrue. This group of people made it sound like our church was the most dangerous place on the face of the earth and characterized the homeless as so many things they're not. Police reports were found and connected to our church even when there was truly no connection. I was smeared publicly, and so was my church community.

As is often the case, people easily believed the lies—not all people, but some people. I was questioned in grocery stores and stopped on my runs in the neighborhood; and I had angry strangers telling me loudly what they thought of me. And the media came. CNN ran the story. It went viral. After it went viral, we got more e-mails. Most were supportive of our mission, but a good chunk of them were derogatory. I was called an expletive for my Latin heritage. Nasty stuff. Degrading to the soul.

All over a simple, compassionate act of feeding the homeless at church.

I learned so much after being lied about. The biggest thing I learned is that when people are smearing you, they don't really want to know the truth; and they certainly don't want to know *your* truth. There's so much energy around the lies that it's a consuming, blinding fire. Sometimes people don't want to know that they are living and spreading a lie.

I learned that sometimes the best response is silence. Sure, you can talk to the media—but for how long? And how much detail do you want to give? And do you really want to spend your life in front of the camera? I watched people argue with me about things that occurred when they weren't even present at the event (and I had been). People can be so certain of their lie that they build an unbreakable wall to protect it. So sometimes silence is the best answer.

And I learned the wisdom of the saying, "In the end, truth rises to the top." I found out that I could rest in the sure knowledge that reputations come and go; but truth is consistent, powerful, and wins in the end. So I didn't have to worry, correct, or chastise.

In Mark 14, there is a hearing before the Sanhedrin. The Sanhedrin was the court, or council, of Israel and was made up of the high priest and seventy other men. They made decisions on matters, much like our city councils do. Jesus was taken to the high priest; and he stood before him and the other chief priests, elders, and lawyers. They were an intimidating group of politically powerful people, and they were looking to expose Jesus as an imposter by hearing testimony against him. They called for people to speak up, and three times they searched for someone to expose Jesus in the public hearing. And three times their efforts failed.

First, the Sanhedrin asked for testimony against him so that they could end his life; but none could be found.

Then some people stepped up and brought false testimony (lies) against Jesus, but this group of people so contradicted themselves that the lies were obvious.

The third time, the Sanhedrin heard some people say that Jesus said that he would destroy the Temple in three days and then build another. But, here again, their testimonies didn't agree on what he actually said. Their testimony couldn't stand up in court.

In Scripture, when something is repeated three times, it means that it is important. Repetition is a literary tool that is still used today, like when Mama counts to three—and you know that she'd better not make it to three or you'll be in for it. Three means hat we need to "sit up and listen to this point, because it matters!" If we didn't know that, we might miss the major mess of lies that are centered in Jesus' death.

Why does it matter that Jesus is being lied about? Because it shows us how much he trusts the truth. Jesus doesn't defend himself. He answers questions directly; but sometimes he just remains silent, watching with a saddened heart as the ones who followed him yesterday are smearing him today.

And it shows us how we, too, can endure a batch of lies with dignity; grace; and yes, with silence. Jesus gave us an example of the suffering servant. Yesterday they loved him. Today they hate him. But Jesus' love for the world didn't change in the midst of a batch of lies.

Finally, the lies let us know that Jesus was sent to his death for a reason other than politics and power. The powerful, politically connected can concoct a plan to kill Jesus; but they can't take away his truth. They can't change who he is: The great I AM is still I AM.

In the end of this passage, the high priest questions Jesus, asking him whether he is the Christ, the Messiah. And Jesus simply says:

> I am. And you will see the Human One sitting on the right
> side of the Almighty and coming on the heavenly clouds.

The answer begins simply, "I am." But it ends powerfully when Jesus places himself on the throne with God Almighty. Jesus is saying that he and God are one. So the Sanhedrin finally found something to charge him with. They charged him with blasphemy, for claiming to be God. And so he was condemned. And he was spat on. And he was beaten. And he was mocked.

Jesus was treated this way because they didn't believe that he was God. Their faith mastered only the mundane understandings of life. They lost their imagination and their awe; and they saw all things as ordinary, which, when you think about it, means that they couldn't believe in the sacred, divine way of being in the world. They limited their lives to what they could understand.

You and I will tell lies sometimes. Sometimes we'll even join in a smear campaign. When we gather around the office coffeepot and share hurtful gossip, we're damaging someone's character, the essence of who they are. When we believe the worst before we believe the best, we're entering into the doorway of lying. When we fail to challenge something we know to be false, or when we fail to listen closely to "the other side," then we close ourselves off to the whole truth.

Jesus, on one of his most awful days, was surrounded by the lies and the liars. And sometimes we can see ourselves in that crowd.

But the word of grace is that we can learn from our mistakes, and we can become truth-tellers. It takes effort, and it takes guarding our mind and our mouths, and it takes determination to live a pure life; but it is possible. It's possible for us to be the voice of truth in our family, our neighborhood, and our churches. It's even possible for our truth to be humbled by the Divine Truth, who knows more than we could ever begin to conceive.

Truth-telling must come at the price of humility. It doesn't come off arrogantly, or self-righteously, or smugly. Truth comes in its truest form as an act of humility. For we know that we know in part when we think of eternity and divinity. We are the human ones, and not *the* Human One; and so we know our place: fully connected to God, but not God. It is our connection that teaches us the truth.

Also, our connection to God is broken when we tell the not-truth to ourselves and to others. Our reliance on God is damaged when we fail to hold truth central.

And so we call ourselves to stand tall in the creation of originality, genuineness, and connection. If you don't know how to make that happen, just take some time to get silent with God, and God will show you how to be. The I AM will show you how to be who you are.

Lying is cowardly. But it takes courage to live in the truth. May your living be full of God's love for your world!

QUESTIONS

1. How is it that Peter is bold enough to follow Jesus into the high priest's courtyard (albeit from a distance)—and even to warm his hands with the guards—yet he denies knowing anything about Jesus just a short time later?

He believes he will support Jesus. Then becomes afraid to do so.

2. What does verse 55 tell us about the fairness of Jesus' trial? Why are the priests so determined to kill Jesus?

Many told lies

Because he says he is the son of God and will be at his right side

3. Why might people have been willing to give false testimony against Jesus? (See verse 57.) Why might we today?

They were afraid

4. Why is Jesus silent in verse 61? Why doesn't he tell his side of the story?

He will not be believed.

5. When someone makes accusations against you, how do you know whether to defend yourself or keep quiet?

Truth will out.

6. Throughout much of Mark, Jesus doesn't seem to want to reveal who he is; yet he makes a bold declaration in verse 62 about his identity to the high priest, which arguably hastens his crucifixion. What has changed? Why now?

He has condemned himself

7. What is the significance of the imagery Jesus uses in verse 62?

Heaven

8. Why does the Sanhedrin consider Jesus' confession of who he is to be an insult against God?

They believe he is lying.

9. Why does the high priest essentially say in verse 63 that no more witnesses are needed?

He said Jesus had insulted God by claiming to be his son

10. Why is there so much hatred and anger expressed against Jesus in verse 65?

Disappointment, anger

11. How should Christians respond to those in society who don't tell the truth? What if those people are other Christians? When are *we* those people?

Hold them responsible but not by violent means

12. In what situations today might God be calling you to step up and defend someone who is the target of someone else's false witness?

Politically

4

BETRAYAL
THE SIN THAT CUTS DEEPEST

SCRIPTURE
MARK 14:10-11, 43-49

[10]Judas Iscariot, one of the Twelve, went to the chief priests to give Jesus up to them. [11]When they heard it, they were delighted and promised to give him money. So he started looking for an opportunity to turn him in.

***

[43]Suddenly, while Jesus was still speaking, Judas, one of the Twelve, came with a mob carrying swords and clubs. They had been sent by the chief priests, legal experts, and elders. [44]His betrayer had given them a sign: "Arrest the man I kiss, and take him away under guard."

[45]As soon as he got there, Judas said to Jesus, "Rabbi!" Then he kissed him. [46]Then they came and grabbed Jesus and arrested him.

[47]One of the bystanders drew a sword and struck the high priest's slave and cut off his ear. [48]Jesus responded, "Have you come with swords and clubs to arrest me, like an outlaw? [49]Day after day, I was with you, teaching in the temple, but you didn't arrest me. But let the scriptures be fulfilled."

INSIGHT AND IDEAS

Who betrayed you? Most of us, when asked this question, are quick to answer. We either know our betrayer right off, or we haven't experienced the pain of betrayal yet. I say, "yet," because, in time, betrayal becomes known in life. It is our common experience; and in turn, it is also our common sin.

The synonyms of *betrayal* are telling. The words *dishonesty, falseness, treachery, deception, unfaithfulness, double-crossing,* and *Judas kiss* are all descriptors of betrayal. The betrayal in the Scripture story is so well known that it makes it into the thesaurus.

Quotations on betrayal also run deep and close. Do you recall these?

> It is easier to forgive an enemy than to forgive a friend.
> —William Blake

> For there to be betrayal, there would have to have been trust first.
> —Suzanne Collins, *The Hunger Games*

Stab the body and it heals, but injure the heart and the
wound lasts a lifetime.
—Mineko Iwasaki

Et tu, Brute?
—Williams Shakespeare, *Julius Caesar*

A true friend stabs you in the front.
—Oscar Wilde

Yet each man kills the thing he loves,
By each let this be heard,
Some do it with a bitter look,
Some with a flattering word,
The coward does it with a kiss,
The brave man with a sword !
—Oscar Wilde, *The Ballad of Reading Gaol*

Betrayal is such a common experience that we can feel
the plunge of the sword in our soul just thinking about it.
Betrayal feels the deepest of pains. The reason betrayal
cuts so deep is that it comes from those we love. Betrayal
happens only close to home. It's one thing to be swindled
by a stranger, but it's something completely different to be
stabbed in the back by a loved one.

As a pastor, I have had a few family members, usually
parents, tell me that their son or daughter did something so
awful that they will never be welcomed in their home again.
When I dig deeper to understand the offense, most times
it is something that truly could be forgiven. But because
it is committed by a loved one, their eyes are clouded by
hurt; and they take the defensive position of not loving,

not being present, and not caring. The "nots" are telling, because the true pain comes from the desire for caring, presence, and love.

The Bible is also filled with stories of betrayal. Remember the stories of

- Samson, whose strength was cut off by his beloved Delilah?

- Joseph, who was sold into slavery by his very own brothers?

- David, who betrayed Bathsheba's husband unto death?

- Gomer, who betrayed Hosea by prostituting their love?

- Jacob, who stole his brother Esau's place of importance?

We can relate to some of these stories. They make us weep. They touch a deep place in our soul as we remember being betrayed by our lover, siblings, and leaders. Everywhere we have the ability to love and trust we open ourselves up for the possible pain of betrayal.

Sometimes we even betray ourselves. We let ourselves down and end up not being able to live with the life we have created. In November 2012, David Oliver Relin, author of the best-seller *Three Cups of Tea,* ended his own life.[1] He had reportedly authored some falsehoods in the book,

---

1 *The Huffington Post* <http://www.huffingtonpost.com/2012/12/03/david-oliver-relin-dead-three-cups-of-tea-coauthor-obituary_n_2229794.html> [Accessed December 3, 2012]

which was meant to raise money to build schools in Central Asia—a good goal gone awry. Earlier in the year, *60 Minutes* and writer Jon Krakauer challenged the facts in the book; and later a lawsuit was filed by four readers. No one, except Relin, knew the depth of pain he faced; but we know that sometimes we all let ourselves down.

Whether betrayal is at the hands of a loved one, or our own doing, the repercussions can be devastating. When we are betrayed, our body shows it. Shoulders stoop. The head looks downward more than upward. The stomach slouches forward. Feet shuffle. Eyes look downcast. External signs of betrayal dress our body when it's really our soul that has been damaged. We lose the confidence, the joy, and the dreams with every Judas kiss.

In the Scripture story, Jesus was the one betrayed. Remember that Jesus chose every one of his disciples. He called them by name. He chose his communal family with deliberation and understanding of their gifts. He chose Judas because Judas cared about the details of money and because he had a passion for the Messiah. I have wondered whether Jesus knew that Judas would betray him when he chose him. Did he choose his betrayer on purpose, knowing the full extent of his plan for life? I'm not sure. In fact, Judas was given great responsibility; and we all know what it means to trust the ones who care for our treasury. They're chosen because they're faithful, accountable, and honest. Judas was all these things.

Yet Judas let his passion get out of control, and he attempted to hasten the events that would cause Jesus to become the King on Earth that Judas had hoped for. Judas let his need to control get out of control, and he set his sight too low for who Jesus was. Jesus wasn't going to be a political power, but rather, an Eternal Presence.

Taking things into his hands, Judas sold his knowledge of Jesus' whereabouts to the enemy. He received funds to betray his beloved friend and master. After a night of wrestling in prayer with God while the other beloved disciples were sleeping through importance, Judas arrived in the Garden of Gethsemane and betrayed Jesus with a kiss of greeting. And as soon as Judas kissed him, Jesus was surrounded by a mob who arrested him. A tussle ensued, and someone cut off the ear of the high priest's slave. Jesus expressed his disgust at all of the use of force and violence, saying:

> Have you come with swords and clubs to arrest me, like an outlaw? Day after day, I was with you, teaching in the temple, but you didn't arrest me. But let the scriptures be fulfilled.
> —Mark 14:48-49

Jesus is saying, "Who do you think I am? Do you think that I am about the fight or the power? Don't you remember me? I'm the one who preached mercy and peace and turn-the-other-cheek. I'm the one who healed your sick child and brought calm to the storm. And today, you come at me with weapons and guards and betrayal? Who do you think I am?"

We betray others when we forget who they really are. We imagine their worst and forget the best, core selves of those we love. That's our problem: We forget.

I love the Holy Communion instruction that says: *Do this in remembrance of me.*

One of the things Jesus wanted us to do most when we are facing difficulties is to remember who he is.

He is the cup of forgiveness and the bread of life. He is truth. He is mercy, grace, and love. And we are called to remember that.

We are placed in the world to remember one another as well as to remember our God. When we know who God is (love) and we remember one another as aspects of God's love, then we are less apt to betray that love. For when we betray one another, we betray God. When we fail to lift up others in their weakness, then we fail to lift up God. When we forget to forgive, then we forget all of the times God has been merciful to us, a sinner. It is in remembrance that we know communion with God and one another.

So to answer the question "Who betrayed you?" is the most courageous act of all. It is to name your pain, the place where someone you loved hurt you deeply. I have an immediate answer to the question. In fact, I have a few answers. Being betrayed is part of life, including mine. But the greater question is, "What do we do with our betrayers?" Do we seek vindication? Do we live in the land of anger and distrust? Do we let our life be taken down a road of distaste because of the reverberations of betrayal? These are questions that matter. Although we will all eventually be betrayed, what we do with our betrayals will make all the difference in our lives.

Jesus said, "Pray for your enemies." Actually, the full text of what he said is as follows:

> You have heard that it was said, *You must love your neighbor and hate your enemy.* But I say to you, love your enemies and pray for those who harass you so that you will be acting as children of your Father who is in heaven. He makes the sun rise on both the evil and the good and sends rain on both the righteous and the unrighteous. If you love only those who love you, what reward do you have? Don't even the tax collectors do the same? And if you greet only your brothers and sisters, what more are you doing? Don't even the Gentiles do the same? Therefore, just as your heavenly Father is complete in showing love to everyone, so also you must be complete.
> —Matthew 5:43-48

So that is what we are called to do as subversive, countercultural, faithful followers of Jesus. We are to pray for those who fail us and love our enemies. Now, you might not be able to conceive of a way to love your enemy yet, but you can probably turn every thought you have for your betrayer to a prayer. "Lord, bring _____ back to the original creation you intended for him, or her." You can whisper, "God, help me forgive and love the one who has hurt me." (Sometimes we have to love from a distance, but that is still love.) You can ask God to release your soul from bitterness, anger, and vindication and replace it with sweetness, understanding, and release.

We ask God to heal us as God heals our betrayer. The two work in tandem. Our healing is intricately connected to our enemy's healing. And that is the mystery of the greatest love of all.

QUESTIONS

1. Judas Iscariot, we're told in verse 10, initiates the arrangement with the chief priests to give Jesus up to them. Besides the money, what else might be a motive for his betrayal?

Perhaps he thought Jesus would declare himself as the savior and became an important leader.

2. Why is it necessary for Judas Iscariot to point out Jesus to the mob? Considering his fame, shouldn't most people have easily recognized Jesus?

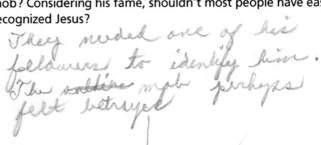

They needed one of his followers to identify him. The soldiers mob perhaps felt betrayed

3. Why do Jesus' followers respond with violence in verse 47?

4. Why does Scripture make it a point in verses 10 and 43 to emphasize that Judas is "one of the Twelve"?

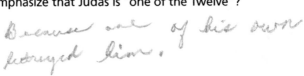

Because one of his own betrayed him.

5. Judas chooses a kiss as the action with which he identifies Jesus to the ones who will arrest him. How does this gesture demonstrate a dichotomy within Judas?

Because he truly loves Jesus and believes Jesus will become an important leader

6. During the Passover meal, Jesus predicts his betrayal; yet he allows Judas to betray him anyway. Why does he do this?

To allow the scriptures to be fulfilled.

7. When are we like Judas in our relationship with God?

When we deny him and do not follow his teachings

8. How can we prevent being betrayed by the ones closest to us? How can we avoid betraying those *we* love?

By having good and honest relationships with those we love

9. Why does betrayal hurt worse when it comes from the people we love most? In what ways can we initiate healing after we've been betrayed?

Because its by those who you love trusted to stand by you. Forgiveness!

EPILOGUE

There's a song, well known and well loved, and most famously sung by Judy Garland, "Over the Rainbow." This place of the rainbow is the place where the best of all dreams come true.

We dream of the land where our common sins aren't so common anymore. We dream of a life without denial, sleepiness, lies, and betrayal. We dream of a place where we understand the lines in the Lord's Prayer:

Our Father, Who art in heaven,
Hallowed be Thy name.
Thy kingdom come, Thy will be done,
On earth, as it is in heaven. . . .

Amen. May it be so today and forever!

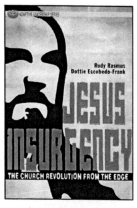
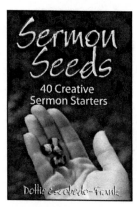

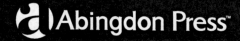

CONVERGE

Bible Studies

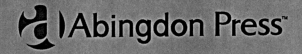

Abingdon Press™

BKM136600001 PACP01354020-01